# Animal Poems

## I Want...

I want a small piece of string with an ant on it carrying a small piece of string with a worm on it carrying a small piece of string with a rhinoceros on it carrying a small piece of string with a horse on it carrying a small piece of string with an elephant on it carrying a small piece of string with a dinosaur on it carrying a small piece of string with a small piece of string on it.

...piece of string with a bird on it carrying a small piece of string with a cat on it carrying a small piece of string with a dog on it carrying a small piece of string with a cow on it carrying a small piece of string with...

Remy Charlip

Other fantastic poetry collections from Scholastic:

*Family Poems*
*Funny Poems*
*Magic Poems*
*Pet Poems*
*School Poems*
*Spooky Poems*

# Animal Poems

Compiled by Jennifer Curry

Illustrated by Anthony Lewis

SCHOLASTIC

This book is for SAM TUBBY,
my enthusiastic and extraordinarily
knowledgeable bird-watching friend.

Scholastic Children's Books,
Commonwealth House, 1-19 New Oxford Street,
London WC1A 1NU, UK
a division of Scholastic Ltd
London ~ New York ~ Toronto ~ Sydney ~ Auckland

First published in the UK by Scholastic Ltd, 1998
This edition published by Scholastic Ltd, 2004

This collection copyright © Jennifer Curry, 1998
Illustrations copyright © Anthony Lewis, 1998

Copyright information for individual poems is given on page 128,
which constitutes an extension of this copyright page.

ISBN 0 439 96855 0

Printed and bound by Nørhaven Paperback A/S, Denmark.

2 4 6 8 10 9 7 5 3 1

# CONTENTS

# SHINING OF THEIR WINGS

## PICTURE POEM

# PREPARE TO SAY OUCH

## PICTURE POEM

## BLUEBOTTLES ON MOTORBIKES

## PICTURE POEM

## OVER A GREEN HEDGE

## PICTURE POEM

# HALF-REMEMBERED FOREST NIGHT

## PICTURE POEM

# LAST WORD

# First Word

## Have You Ever Seen?

Have you ever seen A BAT?
Flitting-flying, sky-diving, brown-skinned,
Ears-listening.

Have you ever seen A CAT?
Slowly-stalking, prey-hunting, eyes-flashing,
Tail-swishing.

Have you ever seen A FOX?
Bushy-tailed, sly-thinking, rusty-colour,
Ever-hungry.

Have you ever seen A SPIDER?
Creeping-crawling, deep-black, legs-sprawling,
Shudder-shivering.

Have you ever seen A PHEASANT?
Long-tailed, brightly-coloured, proud-looking,
Stepping-neat.

Have you ever seen A DEER?
Spotted-black, lightly-walking, swiftly-shy,
Gentle-eyed.

Have you ever?
Have you ever?

– Look inside.

*K. Lampard (12)*

## Homeweb

A COBWEB MAY LOOK MESSY

BUT TO SOME SPI-DER IT IS HOME

*Robert Froman*

12

# I'D RATHER HAVE
# A GERBIL

# The Stick Insect

The stick insect is a delicate grass sculpture,
a wobbling tent frame.
She looks so innocent from far away,
but when you get close, she's fearsome.
Her eyes are mean, a dot of paint, tiger's eyes.
Her jaws are curved, vicious,
but she eats only privet.
Her body is covered with stubble,
   an unshaven face.

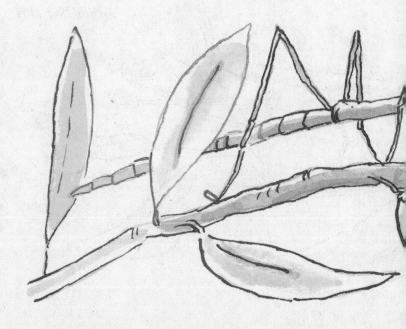

She doesn't move often,
but when she does,
  she moves like an angry boxer,
elbows out, fists forward.
Her skin is like a wrinkled sweet paper,
in segments, like a stack of paper cups.
Knock her leg, and she rears up on one side,
squatting, her leg raised in self-defence.
She doesn't know you're not going to hurt her.

*Andrew Duff (13)*

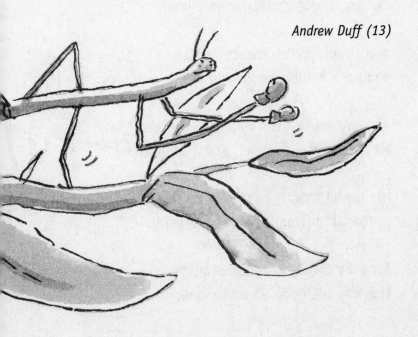

# My Praying Mantis

I once had a mantis as a pet.
A praying mantis, you must not forget,

is the tiger of the insect world,
hungry, fierce and extremely bold;

and if you are an insect, keep away
should a mantis be lurking where you play.

Anyway, my mantis was my very best friend.
He sat on my shoulder, and I did defend

his insect's right to stay with me,
protect him from people's curiosity;

for they thought it very strange
the way his body was arranged:

For a start his neck was very long,
and his heart-shaped head did not belong

to that thin neck and bulbous abdomen
or toothed arms as strong as ten,

wings which gave him speed in flight
when he attacked and with delight

grabbed a cockroach for his supper,
tore and ate it with his choppers.

However, one day, Phoebe, the neighbour's cat,
gobbled up my mantis and that was that.

Phoebe licked her lips, seemed satisfied
with a chewed-up mantis in her inside.

I suppose, for a mantis, the moral to this story
is, look out for cats or you'll be sorry.

*John Lyons*

# A Protest About Cabbage

Our guinea pigs are making
a protest about cabbage.

Each evening we feed them cabbage,
but the cabbage stays uneaten.

They know they can beat us,
each day they lay their plans:

*Okay, when they put us in our run,*
*eat as much grass as you can stomach,*
*fill up with enough to last,*
*then when they throw in the cabbage*
*sit tight, from then on we're on hunger strike.*

Well actually they don't really say it like that,
they use guinea pig speak:

*Squeak, squeak, squeak, squeak grass,*
*squeak, squeak, squeak, squeak lovely.*
*squeak, squeak, squeak, squeak cabbage,*
*squeak, squeak, squeak, squeak YUK!*

Pretty soon we'll stop giving them cabbage
and they know it.

Lettuce and carrot's all right,
but they swoon at the thought of grass.
Grass to a guinea pig is angel delight,
strawberries and cream,
black forest gateaux
and death by chocolate.

But when I tried it – BIG DISAPPOINTMENT!

I don't know what they see in grass,
but I know what they mean about cabbage!

Do you?

*Brian Moses*

# The Tortoise

It creaks along,
In need of oil,
From stone,
To creature.

The cogs grinding,
In the old-fashioned motor.
Plodding patiently,
Head swaying
Rhythmically with its body.

Its shell house
Bumping
Its old wrinkled skin,
As it drags its feet
Along its surroundings.

*Samantha Blamey (11)*

# The Gerbil

"Can we have a gerbil, Mum?"
"We can't," is what Mum said.
"I'm sorry, love," she added.
"I'm having a baby, instead."

"I'd rather have a gerbil, Mum,
I'd like a pet," I said.
But what I'll get is a baby,
With a face all screaming and red.

"I'll tell you what," said Mother,
"I'll tell you what we'll do.
If you help me with the baby,
You can have a gerbil, too."

I got the gerbil I wanted,
And I help Mum every day.
The baby isn't too bad –
But the gerbil's quieter, I'd say.

*Tony Bradman*

# Rabbit Poem

To keep
a rabbit
is a good
habit.

A rabbit is truly curious:
his eyes are soft
but his whiskers wiggle
and his nose twitches
and his ears jiggle

and his tail
is a bump
on
his rump.

A rabbit
is cheerful
but not especially
careful
about multiplying:
the answers
he gets
to the simple
sum
of one and one
are mystifying...

A rabbit is easy
to care for:
to munch on grass
is what he's hare for.

So if you get
the chance
to have a rabbit,
grab it!

*Pamela Mordecai*

# Chicken Dinner

Mama, don' do it, please,
Don' cook dat chicken fe dinner,
We know dat chicken from she hatch,
She is de only one in de batch
Dat de mongoose didn' catch,
Please don' cook her fe dinner.

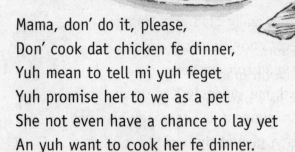

Mama, don' do it, please,
Don' cook dat chicken fe dinner,
Yuh mean to tell mi yuh feget
Yuh promise her to we as a pet
She not even have a chance to lay yet
An yuh want to cook her fe dinner.

Mama, don' do it, please,
Don' cook dat chicken fe dinner,
Don' give Henrietta de chop,
Ah tell yuh what, we could swop,
We will get yuh one from de shop,
If yuh promise not to cook her fe dinner.

Mama, me really glad, yuh know,
Yuh never cook Henny fe dinner,
An she glad too, ah bet,
Oh Lawd, me suddenly feel upset,
Yuh don' suppose is somebody else pet
We eating now fe dinner?

*Valerie Bloom*

# Little White Kitten

Little white kitten
With glass-marble eyes
All springing and leaping
And staring surprise –

Light as a feather
And soft as a puff –
All tiger-cat antics
And dandelion fluff.

*Philip Waddell*

# Our New Arrivals

Snoozing, snuffling, twitching, dreaming,
Our five black puppies
Sleep.

Yawning, stretching, grunting, rolling,
Our five black puppies
Wake.

Jumping, squealing, running, gumming,
Our five black puppies
Play.

Sniffing, sucking, lapping, spilling,
Our five black puppies
Eat.

Snoozing, snuffling, twitching, dreaming,
Our five black puppies
Sleep.

*Oliver Hilton-Johnson (9)*

# My Pony

Over the fields and far away,
My pony and I go out to play.
Elsa's a piebald, nearly six,
She's full of fun and rarely kicks.

She tosses her head and flicks her tail,
And eats her oats from a yellow pail.
She and I are such very good friends,
I hope this friendship never ends.

I love her and she loves me,
And we are one in harmony.
Over the fields and far away,
My pony and I go out to play.

*Rachel Keefe (9)*

# A Flamingo Is

A Flamingo
is
a
long
cooooooooool
drink
of
something
pink

J. Patrick
Lewis

# SHINING OF
# THEIR WINGS

# The A-Z of Bopping Birds

All
Birds
Can
Dance:
Eagles
Foxtrot and
Go-go –
Honest,
It's true!
Jays,
Kookaburras and
Lapwings
Mambo!

**N**uthatches and
**O**wls
**P**ogo!
**Q**uails and
**R**avens
**S**huffle and
**T**wist!
**U**nbelievable, isn't it?
**V**ultures
**W**altz
**X**tra-ordinarily well!
**Y**ellowhammers
**Z**ig-zag!!!!

(okay, okay so I made that one up)

*James Carter*

33

# The Eagle

He clasps the crag with crooked hands;
Close to the sun in lonely lands,
Ringed with azure world, he stands.

The wrinkled sea beneath him crawls;
He watches from his mountain walls,
And like a thunderbolt he falls.

*Lord Tennyson*

# My Christmas Thought

Robin Redbreast
On a silver tree,
Glowing in the moonlight.

*Cherry Hiscox (6)*

# The Sparrow

I found a speckled sparrow
between the showers of rain.

He thought the window wasn't there
and flew against the pane.

I picked him up and held him.
He didn't stir at all.

I hardly felt him in my hand,
he was so soft and small.

I held him like a flower
upon my open palm.

I saw an eyelid quiver,
though he lay still and calm.

And then ... before I knew it
I stood alone, aghast:

I never thought a bird so limp
could fly away so fast!

*Aileen Fisher*

# Swallows

Quick they are
    and slick they are
and swooping through
    the air
as if they couldn't
    stop for joy –
and joy had tossed them
    there.

Loud they are
       and proud they are,
and curving
       as they call,
fly all the way
       from Africa
without a map
       at all.

*Jean Kenward*

# Starlings

This cold grey winter afternoon
The starlings
On the television aerial
Look like sultanas
On a stalk.

*Lucy Hosegood*

# A Poem to Emus

The problem with keeping some emus
Is telling which ones are the she'mus.
They all have long legs,
But, only one lays the eggs.
Those that don't are obviously he'mus.

*David Whitehead*

# The Ladybird
## (with apologies to Clive Sansom)

Tiniest of tortoises,
Your shining back
Is like an egg of red
With spots of black.

How lightly you walk
Across this land
Of valleys and crevasses
That is my hand.

Your tiny black legs
Are small and thin,
Their touch is like feather
Upon my skin.

There, spread out
Your wings and fly.
No frailer creature
Beneath the sky.

*Leoma Rushton (9)*

# A Dragonfly

When the heat of the summer
Made drowsy the land,
A dragonfly came
And sat on my hand,

With its blue jointed body,
And wings like spun glass,
It lit on my fingers
As though they were grass.

*Eleanor Farjeon*

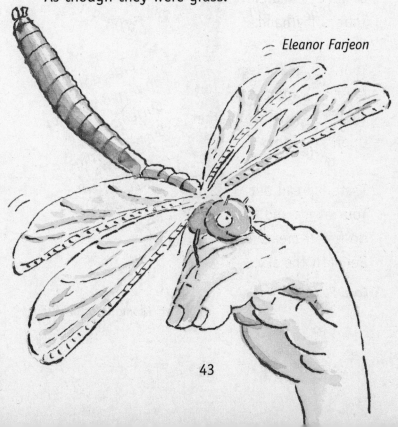

## Patterning

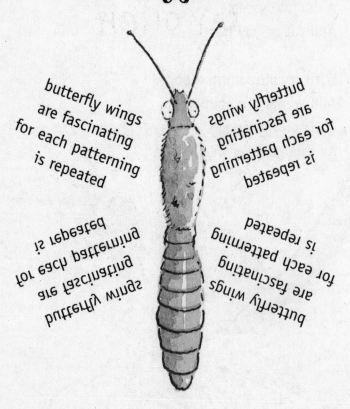

butterfly wings
are fascinating
for each patterning
is repeated

butterfly wings
are fascinating
for each patterning
is repeated

butterfly wings
are fascinating
for each patterning
is repeated

butterfly wings
are fascinating
for each patterning
is repeated

*Coral Rumble*

# PREPARE TO
# SAY OUCH

# Wasps

Wasps like coffee.
Syrup.
Tea.
Coca-Cola.
Butter.
Me.

*Dorothy Aldis*

# ABQ

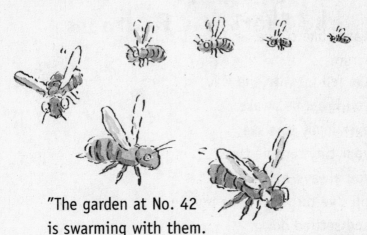

"The garden at No. 42
is swarming with them.

They've all made a beeline for it
and ABQ has been formed.

It's likely to be several hours
before those at the back
reach the flowers.

This is Beattie Blee
for the BBC
outside No. 42 Bielby Road."

*Bernard Young*

# Message for the Mosquito who shares my Bedroom

I'm fed up with the way
you keep me awake
ever ready to slake
your tiny terrible thirst.
You always wait
till I've turned off the light
and settled down
for a good night's zizz
before you start up
that irritating whine.
Announcing, "Mr Mosquito is
out for a bite."

At any second
I might expect to feel
you puncture my skin
and suck my blood.
Tiny vampire,
I am not your personal
tomato ketchup bottle.
If I find you settled
I'll swat you flat.
Be warned of that –
go pester some other
sauce of blood.

*Pie Corbett*

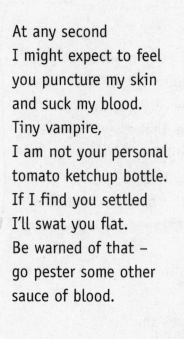

# It's a Dog's Lice
# Being a Head Louse

"Dear Parents,
     May we remind you to see that your
son/daughter thoroughly brushes and
combs his/her hair every night. This will
injure any head lice that they may have
picked up during the day – injured lice do
not survive to lay their eggs."

*(from a school note)*

It's not very nice
being head lice
the teachers just want us snuffled.
We can't lay our eggs,
because your comb broke our legs
when we were warm as fleas in a duffle.

Being a louse
you could lose your house
when the school nurse attacks you with lotions.
And when you comb your hair
you give us a scare
and restrict all our nasty motions.

We pay a high price
for being head lice
it's true that it's tough at the top.
We're just barely alive,
how can we survive
when hair care makes sure that we drop!

*John Rice*

# Don't Call Alligator Long-Mouth Till You Cross River

Call alligator long-mouth
call alligator saw-mouth
call alligator pushy-mouth
call alligator scissors-mouth
call alligator raggedy-mouth
call alligator bumpy-bum
call alligator all dem rude word
but better wait
           till you cross river.

*John Agard*

# The Panther

The panther is like a leopard,
Except it hasn't been peppered.
Should you behold a panther crouch,
Prepare to say Ouch.
Better yet, if called by a panther,
Don't anther.

*Ogden Nash*

# Song of a Bear

There is danger where I move my feet.
I am a whirlwind.
There is danger where I move my feet.
I am a grey bear.
When I walk, where I step lightning flies from me.
Where I walk, one to be feared.
Where I walk, long life.
One to be feared I am.
There is danger where I walk.

*Navajo, North American Indian*

# Mosquito

Mozzie
e
e
e
e
e
e
e
e

e
e
e
e
e
e
e

e
e e
e
e
e e
e
e
e
e e
e
e
e
e
e
e
e
e

*Marie Zbierski*

# BLUEBOTTLES
# ON MOTORBIKES

# Fly-By-Nights

Bats are beautiful.
*Tiny mice with wings*
*that sing*
*as they fly past your head.*

Don't be scared.
*They are only*
*plucking night flies*
*out of the air.*

*Patricia Leighton*

# The Day of the Gulls

On a silver-cold day
Under snow-heavy clouds
The seagulls come
Driven inland
Swooping and screaming
Over the scraps in the gutters.

The children stare
As the street is made beautiful
By the white shining
Of their wings.

*Jennifer Curry*

# Winter

When icicles hang by the wall
  And Dick the shepherd blows his nail,
And Tom bears logs into the hall,
  And milk comes frozen home in pail;
When blood is nipt, and ways be foul,
Then nightly sings the staring owl
              Tuwhoo!
Tuwhit! tuwhoo! A merry note!
While greasy Joan doth keel the pot.

When all around the wind doth blow,
   And coughing drowns the parson's saw,
And birds sit brooding in the snow,
   And Marian's nose looks red and raw;
When roasted crabs hiss in the bowl –
Then nightly sings the staring owl
             Tuwhoo!
Tuwhit! tuwhoo! A merry note!
While greasy Joan doth keel the pot.

*William Shakespeare*

61

# Summer

Summer smells like...
Pot pourri and the bunches of daisies
Peeping out of the rich grass,
Green with goodness.
It fills your lungs and makes you gasp.
And the dog puts his nose into the breeze
And closes his eyes.
The warm smell of rabbits alerts him.
He races, transformed into a greyhound.
You can't stop him now.

I run after him.
He stops, puts his nose into the silent breeze...
Suddenly, a burst of energy
And he leaps into action!
I can't see him anywhere.
Suddenly two ears pop out of the field,
Where wild flowers grow.
He is running, barking,
Sniffing the fragrance that flows out of them.

*Justin Bloomfield (12)*

# Jazzz Does a Dance

Jazzz does a dance
down the street.
He calls it the
soft paw shuffle.

1 – 2 – 3 gliiide.
1 – 2 – 3 purrr.
1 – 2 – 3 smooth.

1 – 2 – 3 YOWL.

There'sthatmadalsatian
andit'schasingme
1 2 3 4 5 6 7
all-the-way-up

this tree.

*Dave Ward*

# from... The Pied Piper
# of Hamelin

Rats!
They fought the dogs, and killed the cats,
And bit the babies in the cradles,
And ate the cheeses out of the vats,
And licked the soup from the cooks' own ladles,
Split open the kegs of salted sprats,
Made nests inside men's Sunday hats,
And even spoiled the women's chats,
By drowning their speaking
With shrieking and squeaking
In fifty different sharps and flats.

*Robert Browning*

# Of Evening in the Wintertime

Of evening in the Wintertime
I hear the cows go home
mooing and lowing by the window
in the muddy loam.

In other places other children
look up and find no stars:
they see tall walls and only hear
buses and motor cars.

I love the muddy lane that lies
beside our lonely house.
In bed I hear all that goes by –
even the smallest mouse.

*George Barker*

# Bluebottles

I hate
bluebottles on motorbikes
when I'm trying to sleep,
especially the big one
in the army jeep.

*Tim Pointon*

# The Honey Pot

*Alan Riddell*

# OVER A GREEN HEDGE

# Badger Watching With Gran

Black all over
Two white stripes on his forehead
Triangly shaped head
Oval shaped body
Sharp claws
Furry
White at the tip of his tail
It's a badger!

*Sam Henry (7)*

# H25

Hedgehogs hog the hedges,
roadhogs hog the roads:
I'd like to build a motorway
for badgers, frogs and toads,
with halts for hungry hedgehogs
at an all-night service station;
four lanes wide and free from man
right across the nation.
Free from oil and petrol fumes,
and free from motor cars,
to see the busy hedgehogs trot
underneath the stars.

*Adrian Henri*

# Anne and the Fieldmouse

We found a mouse in the chalk quarry today
In a circle of stones and empty oil drums
By the fag end of a fire. There had been
A picnic there: he must have been after the crumbs.

Jane saw him first, a flicker of brown fur
In and out of the charred wood and chalk-white.
I saw him last, but not till we'd turned up
Every stone and surprised him into flight,

Though not far – little zigzag spurts from stone
To stone. Once, as he lurked in his hiding-place,
I saw his beady eyes uplifted to mine.
I'd never seen such terror in so small a face.

I watched, amazed and guilty. Beside us suddenly
A heavy pheasant whirred up from the ground,
Scaring us all; and, before we knew it, the mouse
Had broken cover, skimming away without a sound,

Melting into the nettles. We didn't go
Till I'd chalked in capitals on a rusty can:

*Ian Serraillier*

# Vegetarian

I looked over a green hedge
Into a field
And saw a cow.
She looked back at me,
Lips going clockwise
Rhythmically.
Peaceful.
Her eyes were moist,
Her eyelashes fine white threads of silk.
I said:
"Hello cow.
Thanks for the bottles of milk."

She lowered her head
Modestly,
Pulled up a gobbet of grass;
Decided to let my compliment pass.

"And the burgers," I said.

The cow looked up, slowly,
Stopped chewing,
Gazed at me, shaking her heavy head,
But
"You wouldn't begin one
If you knew what was in one,"
Were all the words she said.

*Dee Turner*

# Sheep in Winter

The sheep get up and make their many tracks
And bear a load of snow upon their backs,
And gnaw the frozen turnip to the ground
With sharp quick bite, and then go noising round
The boy that pecks the turnips all the day
And knocks his hands to keep the cold away
And laps his legs in straw to keep them warm
And hides behind the hedges from the storm.
The sheep, as tame as dogs, go where he goes
And try to shake their fleeces from the snows,
Then leave their frozen meal and wander round
The stubble stack that stands beside the ground,
And lie all night and face the drizzling storm
And shun the hovel where they might be warm.

*John Clare*

# Gigl

a pigl
wigl
if
u
tigl

*Arnold Spilka*

# The Donkey

I saw a donkey
One day old,
His head was too big
For his neck to hold;
His legs were shaky
And long and loose,
They rocked and staggered
And weren't much use.

He tried to gambol
And frisk a bit,
But he wasn't quite sure
Of the trick of it.
His queer little coat
Was soft and grey,
And he curled at his neck
In a lovely way.

He looked so little
And weak and slim,
I prayed the world
Might be good to him.

*Anon*

# Horses

Horses stand up still on the skyline,
Waiting for something to happen;
Strangely thoughtful with big sad eyes,
Watching the rain fall mistily,
The clouds move, or just the distance
Escaping from them.
Horses gallop sometimes – up hills,
Across fields, thundering wild,
In a mad explosion of power;
Hot, steaming, violently animal,
But specially, individually horse.
They flail the air and the ground,

Hard-stiff on legs bone-right
And solid-hooved of nail and iron.
They fetlock thrash the tufts of grass and hair,
Rioting down bone and sinew,
Hurrying to be there.
Gigantically gentle with children,
They feel friendly to the touch,
And take sugar quietly.
Stallion-proud and still they look back
To their primeval youth.
They have learned to be patient.

*Paddy Kinsale*

# snail

The tail of the snail tucks round in a bow where well in its shell it baffles the foe.

*David Poulter*

# SMALL, SMALLER

# Worm's-Eye-View of the F.A. Cup Final

"That's funny," said the worm
as it went under Wembley.
"I wonder why the ground's
so loud and trembly."

*Tony Mitton*

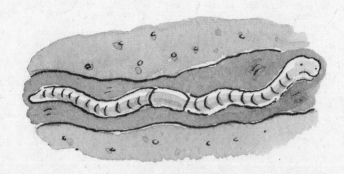

# Only My Opinion

Is a caterpillar ticklish?
  Well, it's always my belief
That he giggles, as he wiggles
  Across a hairy leaf.

*Monica Shannon*

# Ants

Left,
Left, left right left.
Platoon halt,
Pick up cocoons
And forward march.
Come on, save the cocoons.
Down the tunnel
Quick march.
Platoon at ease,
Cocoons down.
About turn.
Forward march
To the food supply,
Pick up food
And back to barracks.
Watch out for air attacks by humans
And that deadly spray.
Left,
Left, left right left.

*Neil Fairweather (11)*

# slug

Shloup shlugal shlobsh shlip
Sligoosh skigoosh shligalop
Shiligigoloshlob skibablosh
Bleshoposlopsh

Puff! Pant! Nearly at the end of the cabbage leaf
Ah, time for another shlogoly bit of cabbage
Shlibylishious,
Oh no, here comes that stupid gardener again!
He must think I'm really stupid
If he thinks I'll eat those disgusting pellets,
Oh no, my sticky shlogy gunge isn't sticky enough
I'm falling,
It's all right, I've landed in the long grass,
It'll take another week to get up on that leaf again
But I'm not in a hurry.

*Jim Bremner (12)*

# Spider on the Toilet

There's a spider on our toilet
Mum says it's big and long,
she says she'll never go again
until the spider's gone.

She says she'll run away
she says she'll never eat,
until the spider,
big and long,
has finished
on our seat.

*Andrew Collett*

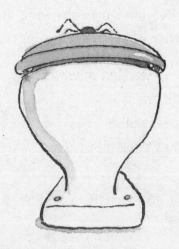

# The Lizard

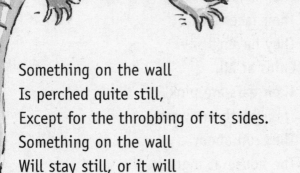

Something on the wall
Is perched quite still,
Except for the throbbing of its sides.
Something on the wall
Will stay still, or it will
Shoot up (or down) very fast.

Something on the wall
Is camouflaged well,
And when it is startled moves away.
Something on the wall
Is a decimetre small,
And sometimes stays for a day.

*Catherine Smart (11)*

# Mice

I think mice
Are rather nice.

    Their tails are long,
    Their faces small,
    They haven't any
    Chins at all.
    Their ears are pink,
    Their teeth are white,
    They run about
    The house at night.
    They nibble things
    They shouldn't touch
    And no one seems
    To like them much.

But *I* think mice
Are nice.

*Rose Fyleman*

# Small, smaller

I thought that I knew all there was to know
Of being small, until I saw once,
   black against the snow,
A shrew, trapped in my footprint, jump and fall
And jump again and fall, the hole too deep,
   the walls too tall.

*Russell Hoban*

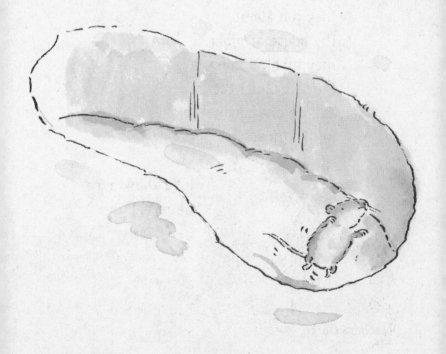

# PICTURE POEM

## Earth-Worm

Do
you
squirm
when
you
see
an earth-worm?
I never
do squirm
because I think
a big fat worm
is really rather clever
the way it can shrink
and go
so small
without
a sound
into the ground.
And then
what about
all
that
work it does
and no oxygen
or miner's hat?
Marvellous
you have to admit,
even if you don't like fat
pink worms a bit,
how with that
thin
slippery skin
it makes its way
day after day
through the soil,
such honest toil.
And don't forget
the dirt
it eats, I bet
you wouldn't like to come out
at night to squirt
it all over the place
with no eyes in your face:
I doubt
too if you know
an earth-worm is deaf, but
it can hear YOU go
to and fro
even if you cut
it in half.
So
do not laugh
or squirm
again
when
you
suddenly
see
a worm.

*Leonard Clark*

92

# A RIPPLE, A WOBBLE, A STIR

# Frogs in Water

There was a splash when the frogs
Jumped in the water.
  A ripple,
  A wobble,
  A stir.
They are deaf to the songbirds
  but
When the rain comes down
And pats the water as if it were a dog,
The frogs gently listen.

*Andrew Abbott (10)*

# It's A:

swift mover
water groover
silent glider
river hider
deep-sea diver
net skiver
trawler's labour
chips' neighbour
silver swimmer
cat's dinner
battered finger
vinegar bringer
Friday's dish
it's a...

*Ann Bonner*

# Ducks' Ditty

All along the backwater,
Through the rushes tall,
Ducks are a-dabbling,
Up tails all!

Ducks' tails, drakes' tails,
Yellow feet a-quiver,
Yellow bills all out of sight
Busy in the river!

Slushy green undergrowth
Where the roach swim –
Here we keep our larder,
Cool and full and dim.

Every one for what he likes!
*We* like to be
Heads down, tails up,
Dabbling free!

High in the blue above
Swifts whirl and call –
*We* are down a-dabbling,
Up tails all!

*Kenneth Grahame*

# The Eel

I don't mind eels
Except at meals:
And the way they feels.

*Ogden Nash*

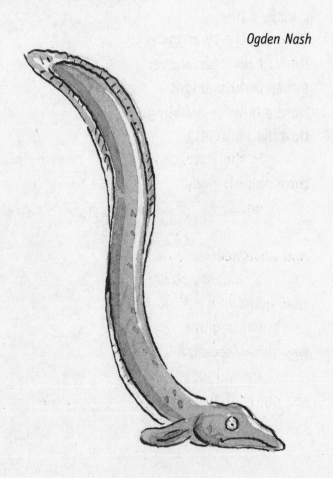

# The Reflection

Down on the river today
  I saw
a huge, white sailing
  swan
pushing his feet
  in the water, and
thrusting his body
  on...

And underneath,
  a shadowy shape
that fitted him
  like a glove
was softly, secretly
  travelling:
the ghost of the swan
  above.

*Jean Kenward*

# Albatross

Hush ... hush ... hush...
The grey wind comes with a rush,
The cold wind comes with a wail,
And gliding across
The gale full sail
Lo! the Albatross.
The wind is her father,
The sea her mother,
She was born in a lather
Of foam and a smother
Of snow, long ago,
Before the ice was old.
She is careless and calm, and as cold
As a fleece of snow,
She is lovely and large, and as lone
As the Arctic Zone.
The wind
And the sea
Between them toss
Their daughter, the Albatross.

*Eleanor Farjeon*

# Penguin

Big flapper
Belly tapper
Big splasher
Fish catcher
Beak snapper.

*Rebecca Clark (8)*

# The Sea Otter

The sea otter lives where the icebergs swarm,
But his thick fur coat keeps him beautifully
  warm.
He dives in the water for crabs and fish,
For the otter thinks crabs are an excellent
  dish;
And it's terribly useful when you are able
To use your fur tummy instead of a table.

*Alison Jezard*

# Seal

Swiftly and quickly
he dives from the ice,
Down under the water
in a trice,
In and out of his watery room
He zips past the fish
with a playful zoom.
With a mouthful of fish
he swims to the top,
and lands on the ice
with a delicate plop.

*Lyn Melandri (10)*

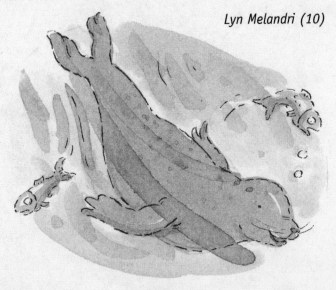

# The Whale's Hymn

In an ocean before cold dawn broke
Covered by an overcoat
I lay awake in a boat
And heard a whale.

Hearing a song so solemn and so calm
It seemed absurd to feel alarm –
But I had a notion it sang
God's favourite hymn,

And spoke direct to Him.

*Brian Patten*

# An Alligator I Saw in Florida

I'm full of fish,
  feel quite replete.
What could be better
  than to dangle my feet
in cool, cool water?
  Hey, man,
      this
              is
                  neat.

I'm watchful, though.
  My slit-eyed gaze
warns I'm not totally
  lost in dreamy haze.
On this rock I bask.
  Ummmm, man,
      I love
          long
              lazeee
                  days!

*Wes Magee*

# The Hippopotamus

Consider the poor hippopotamus:
His life is unduly monotonous.
He lives half asleep
At the edge of the deep,
And his face is as big as his bottom is.

*Anon*

*A little boy in my wife's class looked
at a jar of frogspawn and said:
"Cor – look at that FROGS BORN."
I think he had the best word.*

## Frogspawn

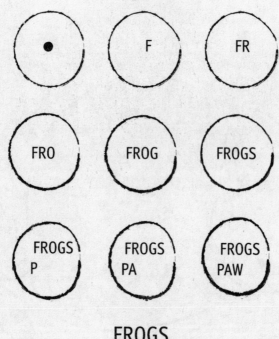

FROGS
BORN!!

*Peter Dixon*

# HALF-REMEMBERED
# FOREST NIGHT

# Night Prowler

Skulking round the dustbins,
Flame-red in dead of night,
Sharp-pricked ears, dark plume of a tail –
Urban fox on the back street trail.

*Jennifer Curry*

# The New Gnus

A gnu who was new to the zoo
Asked another gnu what he should do.
The other gnu said, shaking his head,
"If I knew, I'd tell you, I'm new too."

*John Foster*

# Grey Squirrels

Some people may consider these animals
   attractive
but, in many places, like the one where I live,
the species has become a threat, each creature
   hyper-active.

Squirrels learn things fast. Through any open
   window they climb in
to find the larder, knock glasses from the shelf
   and raid the bread bin,
where they fight to get the lid off, kicking up
   a dreadful din.

Sometimes a pair of silky young ones have
   been found
sleeping in the corn bin, having eaten through
   the lid without a sound,
tails furled on palpitating stomachs, full and
   round.

When I go out, they set about the poultry
   house for food,
nibbling slowly through the wire netting.
   So I know a squirrel could
chew a hole in almost anything, in time; and
   they love wood.

So I gave in, and now I feed them – cold
   spaghetti, old pork pies,
which they hold neatly, munching quickly,
   with surprise
portrayed in every quivering whisker of their
   tails, and cheeky eyes.

*Jane Whittle*

# The Sloth

The sloth may smile,
The sloth may frown.
It's hard to tell –
he's upside down!

*Colin West*

# Iguana Memory

Saw an iguana once
when I was very small
in our backdam backyard
came rustling across my path

green like moving newleaf sunlight

big like big big lizard
with more legs than centipede
so it seemed to me
and it must have stopped a while
eyes meeting mine
iguana and child locked in a brief
split moment happening
before it went hurrying

for the green of its life

*Grace Nichols*

# I Wannabe a Wallaby

I wannabe a wallaby,
A wallaby, that's true.
Don't wannabe a possum,
A koala or a 'roo.

I wannago hop-hopping
Anywhere I please,
Hopping without stopping
Through eucalyptus trees.

A wallaby, a wallaby,
That is what I wannabe.
I'd swop my life to be one,
But a problem I can see;

If I'm gonna be a wallaby
I shall have to go and see
If I can find a wallaby,
A very friendly wallaby,
Who would really, really, really ...

Wannabe ME!

David Whitehead

# The Polar Bear

The polar bear's
fur is
like sugar.
His nose
is like a
black plum.

*Jason Fields (9)*

# The Lion

The lion has a golden mane
and under it a clever brain.
He lies around and idly roars
and lets the lioness do the chores.

*Jack Prelutsky*

# Elephantasia

If an elephant wore big rubber boots –
    Would it be a Wellyphant?

Or if one was raspberry red and wobbly –
    Could it be a Jellyphant?

If you saw one on a TV show –
    Might it be a Telephant?

What if an elephant never had a shower –
    Would he be a Smellyphant?

Or if one got so very, very fat –
     Might we say – Pot-bellyphant?

Do you think we'll ever, ever know?

     No, not on your Nelly-phant!

*David Whitehead*

# Tiger and Wolf

Tiger
Tiger, eyes dark with
half-remembered forest night,
stalks an empty cage.

Wolf
still on his lone rock
stares at the uncaged stars and
cries into the night.

*Judith Nicholls*

# The Tiger

The tiger has wise eyes.
He knows about men.
They put traps to kill him.
They will take his coat for
rich ladies to wear.
The tiger is angry.
So am I.

*Vorakit Boonchareon (5)*

# Tall Story

my

on

it

fit

not

could

but

giraffe,

a

measure

to

went

I went to measure a giraffe, but could not fit it on my

graph

*Mike Johnson*

# Last Word

## The Deers' Request

We are the disappearers.
You may never see us, never,
But if you make your way through a forest
Stepping lightly and gently,
Not plucking or touching or hurting,
You may one day see a shadow
And after the shadow a patch
Of speckled fawn, a glint
Of a horn.
  Those signs mean us.

O chase us never. Don't hurt us.
We who are male carry antlers
Horny, tough, like trees,
But we are terrified creatures,
Are quick to move, are nervous
Of the flutter of birds, of the quietest
Footfall, are frightened of every noise.

If you would learn to be gentle,
To be quiet and happy alone,
Think of our lives in deep forests,
Of those who hunt us and haunt us
And drive us into the ocean.
If you love to play by yourself
Content in that liberty,
Think of us being hunted,
Tell those men to let us be.

*Elizabeth Jennings*

Acknowledgements

The compiler and publishers would like to thank the following for permission to use copyright material in this collection. The publishers have made every effort to contact the copyright holders but there are a few cases where it has not been possible to do so. We would be grateful to hear from anyone who can enable us to contact them so that the omission can be corrected at the first opportunity.

Bantam, Doubleday Dell Publishing Group Inc. for "Only My Opinion" by Monica Shannon from *Goose Grass Rhymes* ~ Valerie Bloom for "Chicken Dinner" from *Duppy Jamboree*, pub. Cambridge University Press ~ Ann Bonner for "It's A:" from *My First Has Gone Bonkers*, pub. Blackie ~ Tony Bradman for "The Gerbil" ~ Calder Publications Ltd for "The Honey Pot" by Alan Riddell from *Eclipse* ~ James Carter for "The A-Z of Bopping Birds" ~ Robert Clark for "Earth-Worm" by Leonard Clark ~ Andrew Collett for "Spider on the Toilet" ~ Pie Corbett for "Message for the Mosquito..." from *Mrs Noah's Notebook*, pub. OUP ~ Curtis Brown Ltd for "Iguana Memory" by Grace Nichols ~ Jennifer Curry for "The Day of the Gulls" and "Night Prowler" from *Down Our Street*, pub. Methuen ~ David Higham Associates for "A Dragonfly" and "Albatross" by Eleanor Farjeon from *Silver, Sand and Snow*, pub. Michael Joseph. "Small, Smaller" by Russell Hoban from *The Pedalling Man and Other Poems*, pub. Heinemann ~ Peter Dixon for "Frogspawn" ~ Aileen Fisher for "The Sparrow" from *Feathered Ones and Furry*, pub. Thomas Y Cromwell, New York ~ John Foster for "The New Gnus" from *A Fifth Poetry Book*, pub. OUP ~ Robert Froman for "Homeweb" ~ Halesworth Middle School for "Summer" by Justin Bloomfield ~ Sam Henry for "Badger Watching With Gran" ~ Elizabeth Jennings for "The Deers' Request" from *Collected Poems*, pub. Carcanet ~ Mike Johnson for "Tall Story" ~ Jean Kenward for "Swallows" and "The Reflection" ~ Patricia Leighton for "Fly-By-Nights" ~ J Patrick Lewis for "A Flamingo Is..." from *A Hippopotamusn't*, pub. Dial Books, 1990 ~ Wes Magee for "An Alligator I Saw..." ~ The Ministry of Education, Victoria, Australia for "Seal" by Lyn Melandri from *The Sea* ~ Tony Mitton for "Worm's-Eye-View..." from *'Ere we go*, pub. Piper/Pan Macmillan ~ Pamela Mordecai for "Rabbit Poem" ~ Brian Moses for "A Protest About Cabbage" ~ Judith Nicholls for "Tiger and Wolf" from *Midnight Forest*, pub. Faber & Faber ~ Brian Patten for "The Whale's Hymn" from *Gargling With Jelly*, pub. Viking ~ Tim Pointon for "Bluebottles" ~ David Poulter for "Snail" ~ GP Putnam's Sons for "Wasps" by Dorothy Aldis from *Is Anybody Hungry?* ~ Random House Children's Books for "The Stick Insect" by Andrew Duff from *Wondercrump Poetry 1*, and Random House Ltd for "The Sea Otter" by Alison Jezard from *The Much Better Story Book* ~ John Rice for "It's a Dog's Lice..." ~ Rogers, Coleridge & White Ltd for "H25" by Adrian Henri from *Dinner With Sprats*, pub. Methuen ~ Routledge & Keegan Paul for "Starlings" by Lucy Hosegood from *Those First Affections* ~ Coral Rumble for "Patterning" ~ The Society of Authors for "Mice" by Rose Fyleman ~ Turning Heads for "The Ladybird" by Leoma Rushton and "The Polar Bear" by Jason Fields from *Cadbury's 3rd Book of Children's Poetry*. "Frogs in Water" by Andrew Abbott from *Cadbury's 4th Book of Children's Poetry*. "The Tortoise" by Samantha Blamey from *Cadbury's 5th Book of Children's Poetry*. "My Christmas Thought" by Cherry Hiscox and "The Lizard" by Catherine Smart from *Cadbury's 6th Book of Children's Poetry*. "Slug" by Jim Bremner from *Cadbury's 7th Book of Children's Poetry*. "Our New Arrivals" by Oliver Hilton-Johnson and "Penguin" by Rebecca Clark from *Cadbury's 9th Book of Children's Poetry*. ~ Philip Waddell for "Little White Kitten" ~ Walker Books for "My Praying Mantis" by John Lyons ~ Dave Ward for "Jazzz Does a Dance" from *Candy and Jazzz*, pub. OUP ~ Colin West for "The Sloth" from *The Best of West*, pub. Random House Children's Books ~ David Whitehead for "A Poem to Emus", "I Wannabe a Wallaby" and "Elephantasia" ~ Jane Whittle for "Grey Squirrels" ~ Bernard Young for "ABQ" from *Double Talk*, pub. Stone Creek Press.